CONTENTS

Foreword

Survival skills have been my foremost proficiency since childhood, forged in the crucible of my birth during the Vietnam-American war in the tumultuous 70s. The echoes of scarcity lingered post the revolutionary year of 1975, where even having enough food was a relentless struggle. This tenacity imprinted survival skills into every facet of my life.

My passion for concept arts seamlessly intertwines with my daily endeavors in digital creation—be it content creation, illustration, or art. The discovery of an AI tool capable of transforming text into images was a revelation. The thrill it brought mirrored the essence of survival, enabling me to swiftly translate ideas into visuals, a testament to my enduring spirit.

As I delved into various tools, a meticulous comparison ensued, revealing the ones that not only economized time but consistently delivered superior results. This book serves as a distilled summary, offering insights into the tools I wish I had known about a year ago, a guide for those navigating the expansive landscape of creative tools, much like the survival skills that have guided me throughout my life.

THE ART OF ALGORITHMS: ENHANCING CONCEPT ARTS WITH AI

CHAPTER 1: INTRODUCTION TO CONCEPT ART AND ALGORITHMS

Concept art and algorithms might seem like two contrasting fields at first glance, with the former being associated with creativity and the latter with logic and computation. However, when combined, these two disciplines can produce truly remarkable results, pushing the boundaries of artistic expression and innovation. In this chapter, we delve into the fascinating world where concept art meets algorithms, exploring the ways they synergize to enhance artistic creations.

Concept art, as the name suggests, is an integral part of the creative process in various industries such as video games, film, and animation. It serves as a visual representation of ideas, providing a glimpse into the world that is yet to be brought to life.

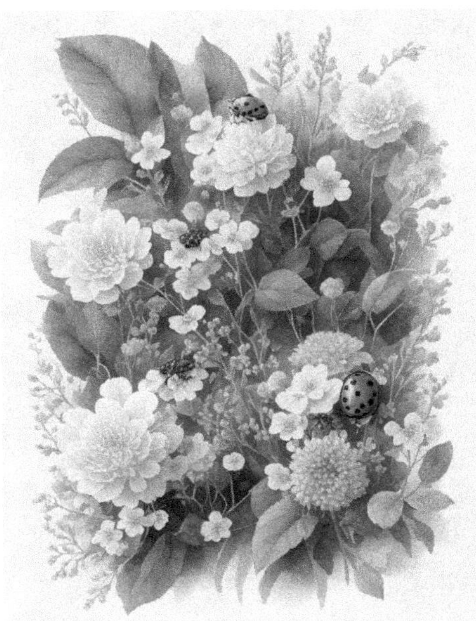

Artists create concept art to develop the overall look, feel, and atmosphere of a project, whether it's designing imaginative characters, breathtaking landscapes, or intricate machinery. These captivating visuals not only inspire other artists involved in the production but also captivate the audience's imagination.

On the other hand, algorithms are the building blocks of computer science and mathematics. They are step-by-step instructions implemented to solve problems or perform specific tasks.

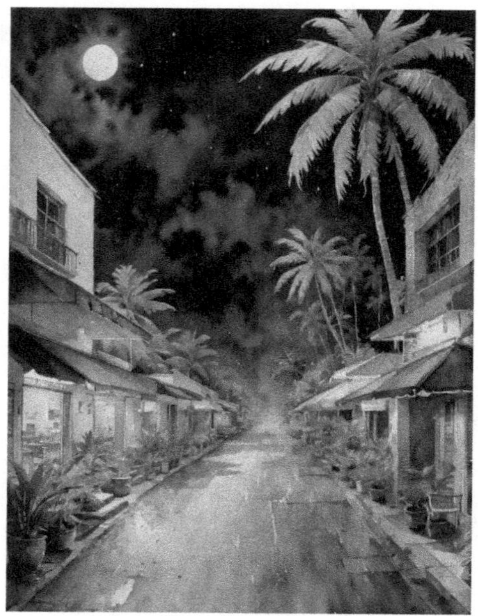

Algorithms are the driving force behind much of the technology we interact with daily, from internet search engines to social media recommendation systems.

They bring order to chaos, enabling computers to process vast amounts of data and generate results at lightning speed.

Algorithms have a reputation for their logical precision and efficiency, making them an invaluable tool in various domains.

Now, what happens when we combine the artistic creativity of concept art with the computational power of algorithms?

The possibilities become boundless. By harnessing algorithms, artists can expand their artistic capabilities and explore uncharted territories.

Algorithms can assist artists by automating repetitive processes, generating complex patterns or textures, and even providing inspiration through random variations.

This fusion of art and algorithms opens up new avenues for artistic expression, enabling artists to achieve results that were previously unimaginable.

For example, one particular application of algorithms in concept art is the generation of landscapes.

Instead of painstakingly drawing every detail of a vast and intricate world, artists can employ procedural generation algorithms to create vast, immersive environments.

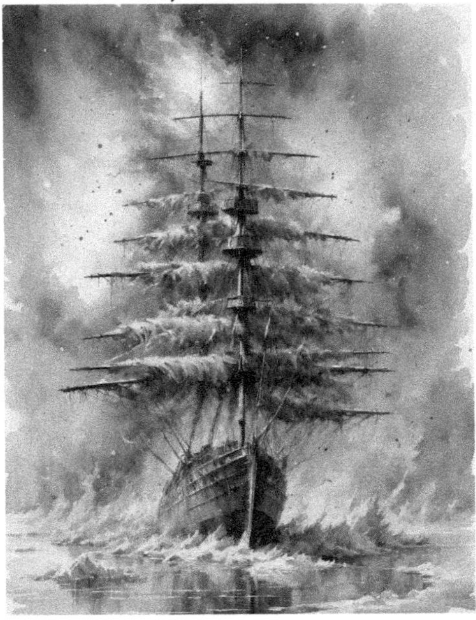

These algorithms use predetermined rules and parameters to generate landscapes that appear natural and diverse, saving artists significant time and effort.

This not only accelerates the creative process but also allows for exploration of endless possibilities, ultimately leading to more visually striking and unique worlds.

Furthermore, algorithms can also be used to enhance the realism and believability of characters in concept art. By employing techniques such as physics simulations or artificial intelligence, artists can imbue their creations with life-like qualities.

Algorithms can dictate realistic movements, simulate natural behaviors, and even generate facial expressions based on emotional states.

This level of realism adds depth and immersion to the concept art, drawing the audience further into the artist's vision.

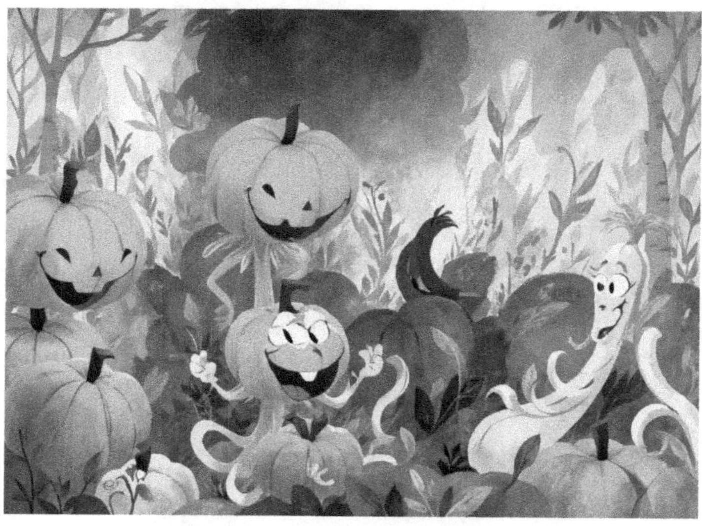

In conclusion, the combination of concept art and algorithms promises to revolutionize artistic creations.

As we continue to explore the intricate relationship between creativity and computation, new opportunities emerge for artists to push the boundaries of their imagination.

The fusion of these two fields results in thought-provoking, visually captivating, and technologically advanced artwork that makes us question what is possible.

In the second half of this chapter, we will dive deeper into specific examples and techniques that demonstrate how these two worlds intertwine seamlessly. Stay tuned for an exploration of the Art of Algorithms.

Now that we have established the potential of combining concept art and algorithms in the first half of this chapter, let us delve deeper into specific examples and techniques that highlight their seamless integration.

By exploring these examples, we can gain a better understanding of how algorithms can elevate the world of concept art to new heights of creative expression and innovation.

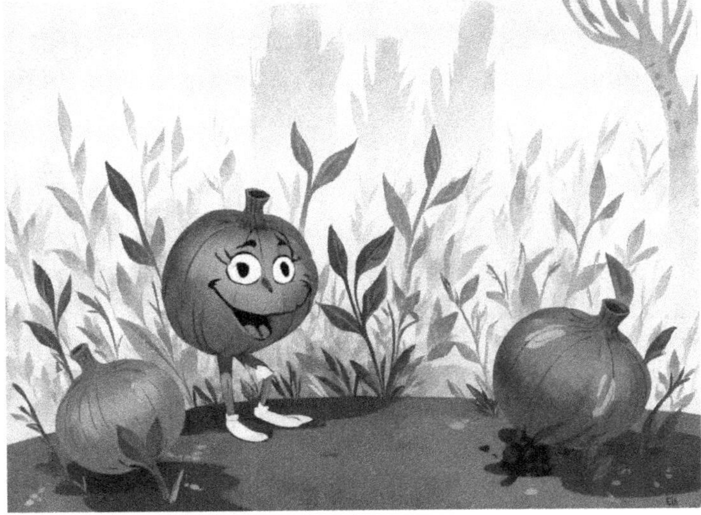

One remarkable application of algorithms in concept art is the generation of realistic and diverse character designs.

Combining the artistic vision of the concept artist with algorithmic techniques allows for the creation of characters with unique traits, appearances, and personalities.

Through the use of procedural generation algorithms, artists can define a set of rules and parameters that govern the generation of characters, resulting in a vast array of possibilities.

These algorithms can take into account factors such as age, gender, race, body proportions, and facial features, among others, to produce visually striking and believable characters.

Not only can algorithms generate character designs, but they can also bring them to life through realistic movement and animation.

By employing physics simulations and motion capture techniques, artists can create characters that move and interact naturally within their virtual environments.

Algorithms can calculate the motion of characters based on their physical attributes, such as weight and flexibility, resulting in fluid and lifelike animations.

This level of realism adds an additional layer of depth and immersion to concept art, making the characters more relatable and believable to the audience.

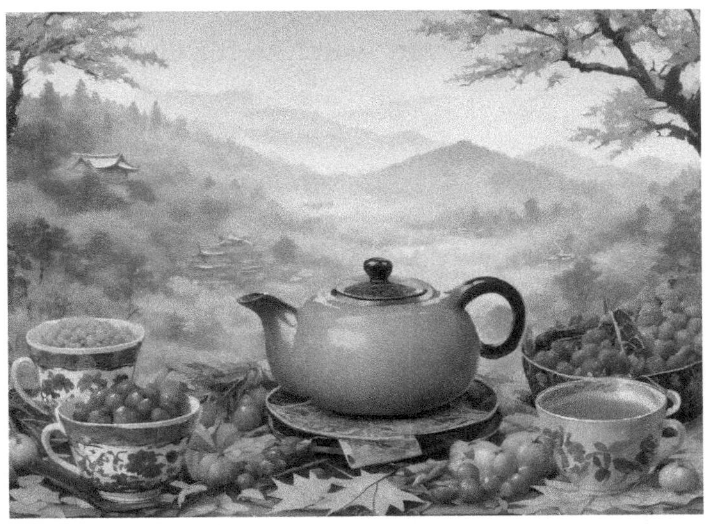

In addition to character design, algorithms can also contribute to the creation of intricate and visually captivating environments.

For example, artists can utilize algorithms to generate complex and realistic cityscapes, forests, or architectural designs.

These algorithms can simulate the growth of cities or the formation of landscapes based on predefined rules, resulting in visually diverse and immersive environments.

By leveraging algorithms, artists can save significant time and effort in designing intricate details, allowing them to focus on the overall artistic vision and storytelling.

Example 1: Sign up and log in Prompt Hunt website, the easiest app I found just after the Gencraft site, they provided themes, styles - you select themes or styles and click CREATE to get a simulated art version, twist and try again go get another version untill it suits you.

Watch the 7 minutes explanation for Prompt Hunt:

https://www.youtube.com/watch?v=f6DCiiaNH_Y

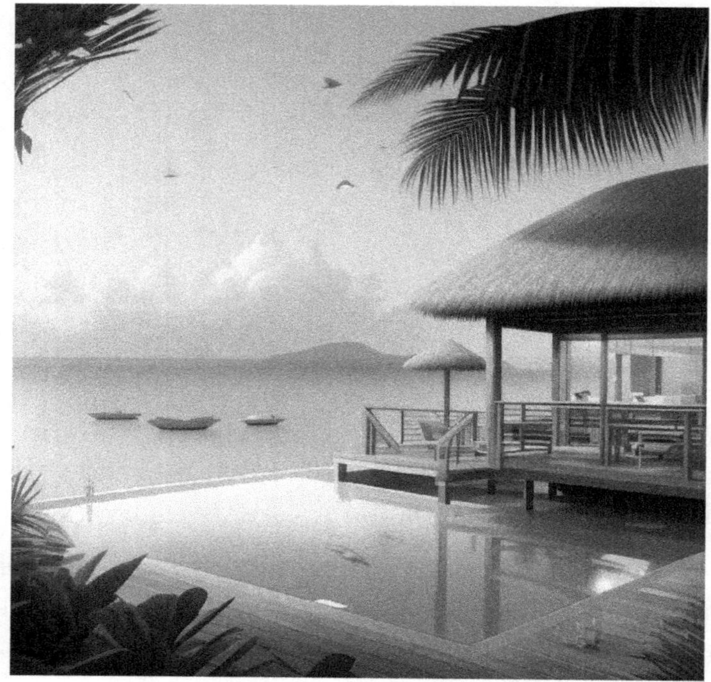

Algorithm simulated V1

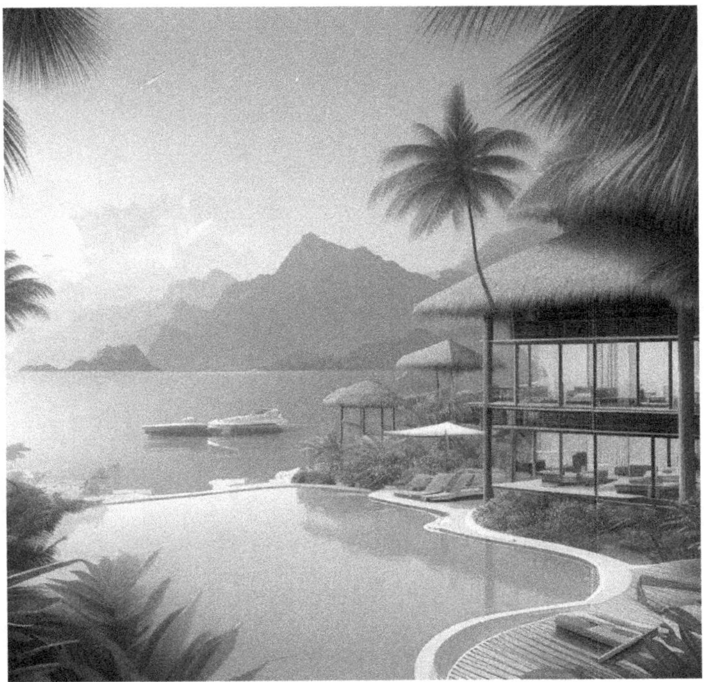

Algorithm simulated V2

How these images were made?

Use the website: https://www.prompthunt.com

Prompts writing idea was taken from this website: https://vitalentum.net/ai/43259.html

Process:

1. Copy the prompts and paste on the prompthunt.com

2. Select theme Doodles, select the shape, click create

3. Click on the pen sign and select Magic enhance to get the simulated image. You can keep clicking the Magic enhance button to get the version that suit your need.

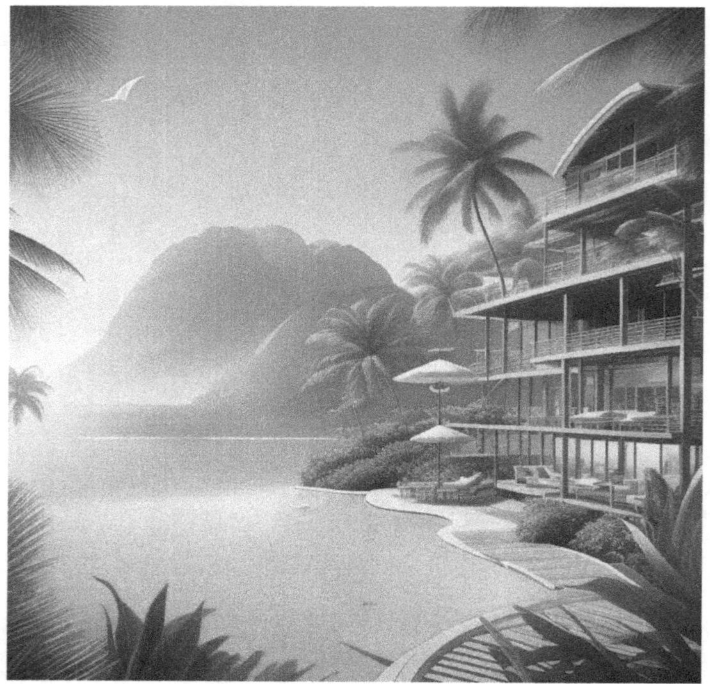

Algorithm simulated V3

Note: the prompt used in this example:

"A serene water resort with a wooden deck, surrounded by marine views. The soft and atmospheric lighting creates a peaceful ambiance. The detailed rendering showcases the beauty of the tropical setting."

Another fascinating aspect where concept art and algorithms intersect is in the creation of textures and materials. Algorithms can be used to generate intricate patterns, simulate the behavior of different types of materials, and even imitate natural phenomena such as weathering or erosion.

By harnessing the computational power of algorithms, in artists can create textures that are both visually appealing and conceptually meaningful. These textures add depth and realism to the artwork, enhancing the overall immersive experience for the audience.

Example 2: Pattern enchanting surrealistic element created by Gencraft, an easy to use app, especially when you need a quick concept art generated in two versions.

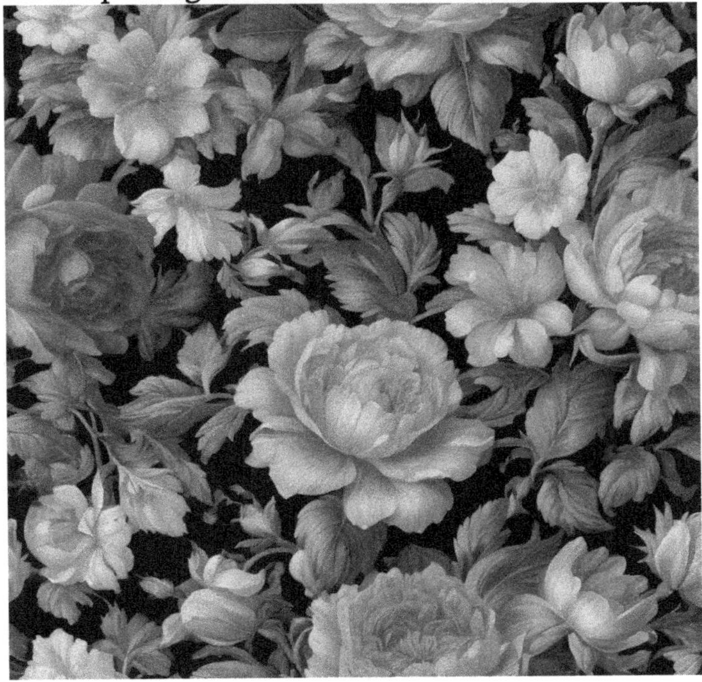

This result comes from the prompt:

"A captivating seamless pattern featuring large flowers in shades of light orange and red. The design is heavily influenced by the Baroque period, with its intricate ornamentation and realistic attention to detail. Despite the realism, there is a whimsical touch to it, adding an enchanting surrealistic element to the pattern."

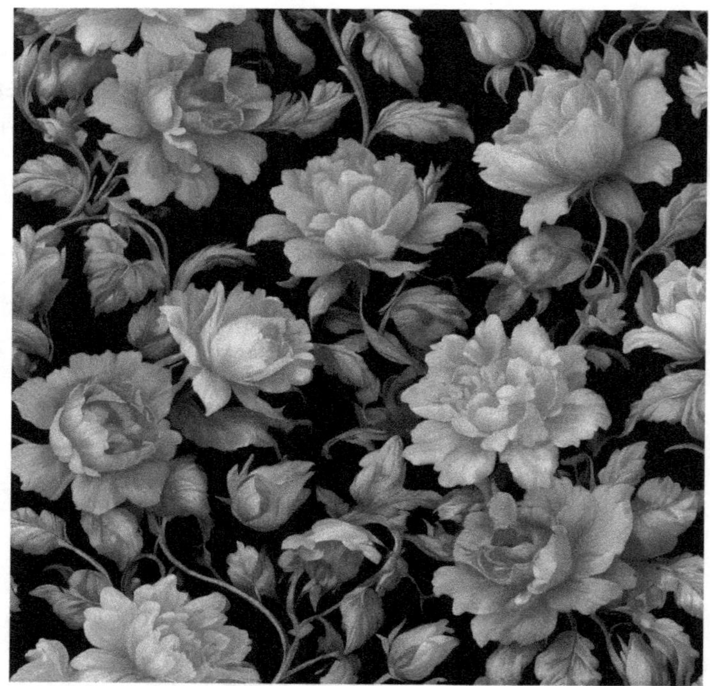

Process:

1. Login gentcraft.com

2. Select Floral style & Image 2.0 default, click generate

Try different styles to experiment different results.

In conclusion, the fusion of concept art and algorithms provides artists with a toolkit that enables them to push the boundaries of their creativity. By leveraging algorithms, concept artists can create unique characters, immersive environments, and visually stunning textures.

The use of algorithms not only enhances the artistic capabilities of the concept artist but also accelerates the creative process, allowing for exploration of endless possibilities.

As we continue to explore the intricate relationship between creativity and computation, it becomes evident that the art of algorithms has the potential to transform the way we perceive and appreciate concept art.

In the next chapter, we will dive even deeper into specific techniques and methodologies that artists can employ to achieve extraordinary results by combining concept art and algorithms.

Stay tuned for an exploration of innovative algorithms and their impact on the artistic realm.

CHAPTER 2: FUNDAMENTALS OF AI AND MACHINE LEARNING

Explore the fundamental concepts of artificial intelligence and machine learning, providing a solid foundation for understanding the role of AI in improving concept arts.

Artificial Intelligence (AI) and Machine Learning (ML) have become buzzwords in recent years, revolutionizing various industries and transforming the way we perceive technology. With their ability to analyze vast amounts of data and learn from patterns, AI and ML have opened up unprecedented possibilities for enhancing concept arts and fostering creativity.

In this chapter, we will delve into the fundamentals of AI and ML, laying a strong groundwork for understanding their significance in the realm of concept arts.

To comprehend the impact of AI and ML on concept arts, it is essential to grasp the basic principles that underpin these technologies. Artificial intelligence refers to the development of computer systems that can perform tasks that typically require human intelligence, such as perception, reasoning, learning, and problem-solving. Machine learning, on the other hand, is a subset of AI that focuses on enabling computer systems to learn and improve from experience without being explicitly programmed.

The core idea behind machine learning is that algorithms can be designed to automatically learn and make predictions or decisions based on data.

This is achieved by training models on large sets of data, allowing them to recognize and generalize patterns, and subsequently using this knowledge to make accurate predictions or provide insights.

Machine learning models can be categorized into supervised learning, unsupervised learning, and reinforcement learning.

Supervised learning involves training a model using labeled examples, where the correct answers are provided alongside the input data.

The model then learns to associate inputs with corresponding outputs, enabling it to make accurate predictions on new, unseen data.

Unsupervised learning, on the other hand, deals with training models on unlabeled data, seeking to discover patterns or structure within the data itself. This approach is often used for clustering or dimensionality reduction tasks. Lastly, reinforcement learning involves training agents to interact with an environment, learning from rewards or punishments to achieve specific goals.

One of the key factors that has contributed to the rapid advancement of AI and ML is the availability of large datasets.

With the exponential growth of digital content, vast

amounts of diverse and labeled data have become accessible, fuelling the development and training of sophisticated machine learning models.

These models are capable of recognizing and generating highly complex patterns, allowing for innovative applications in various domains, including concept arts.

By harnessing the power of AI and ML, artists and designers can augment their creative capabilities and push the boundaries of their imagination.

AI-based algorithms can analyze existing artwork, identify patterns and styles, and generate new ideas that align with the artist's vision. This collaboration between human creativity and AI algorithms can foster a synergy that not only enhances the artistic process but also opens up new avenues for exploration in concept arts.

Example 3: We use this prompt to chunk out 3 designs below.

"A captivating white and blue diner booth, with an exquisite blend of light red and dark aquamarine. The tabletop photography captures the essence of Chicago imagists with its ornate and distinct stylistic range. Inspired by the Glasgow style, this piece elevates mundane materials into a captivating masterpiece."

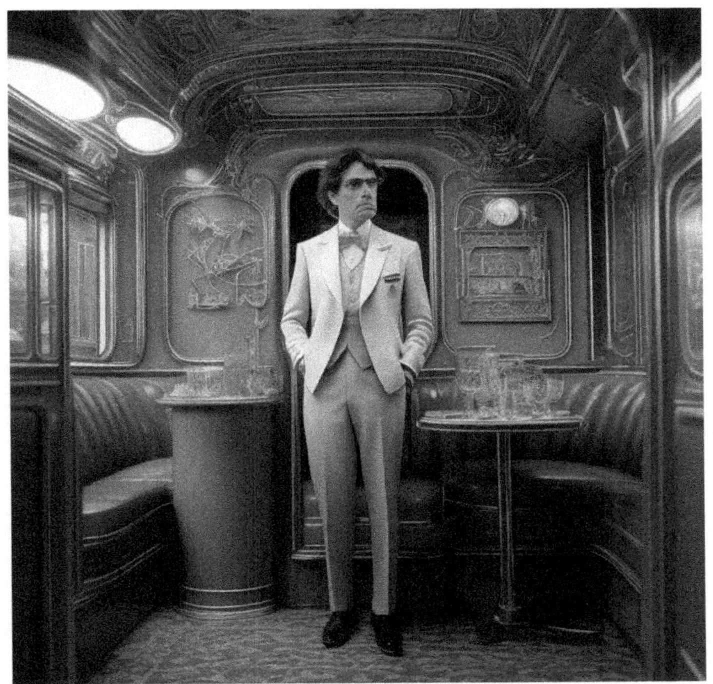

boundary of imagination v1

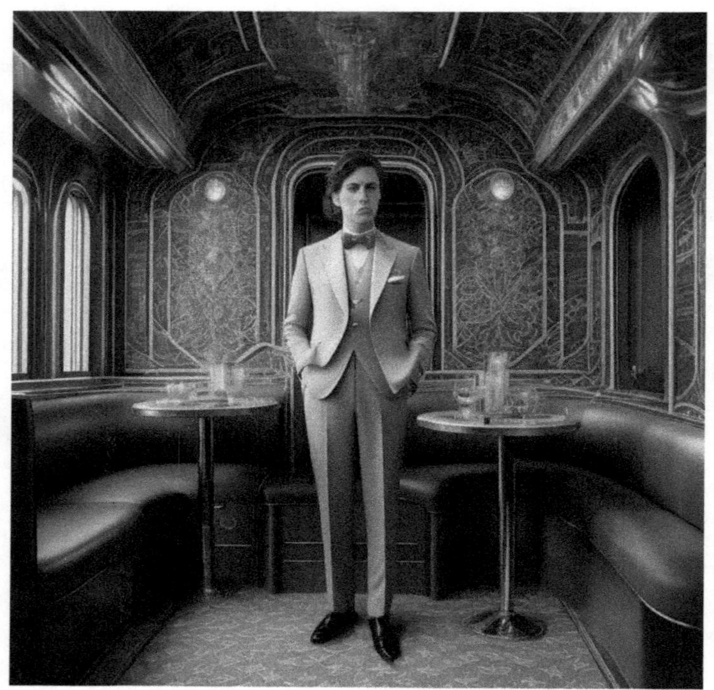

boundary of imagination v2

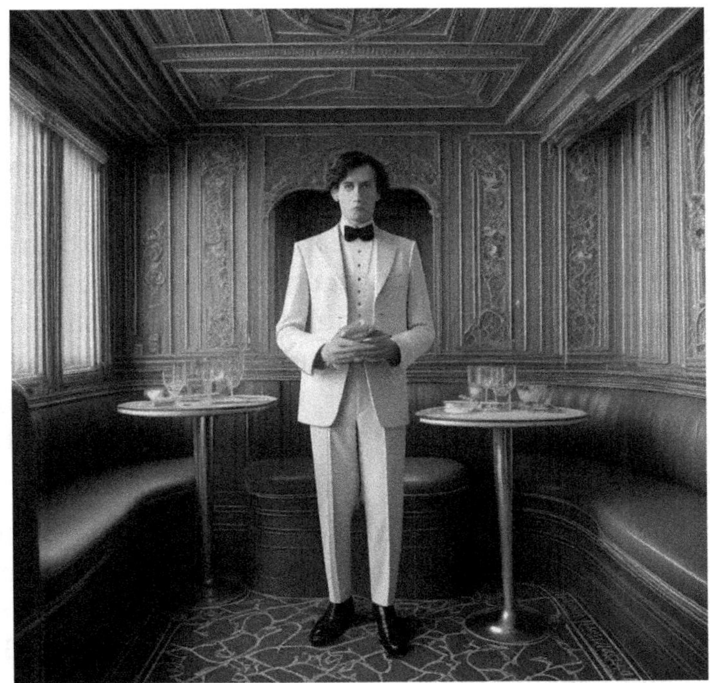

boundary of imagination v3

These cutting-edge approaches have revolutionized the creative process, allowing artists and designers to push the boundaries of their imagination and bring their visions to life. Through AI-assisted concept arts, the fusion of human creativity and machine learning has unlocked new avenues of exploration and sparked innovative ideas.

One of the fascinating techniques employed in concept arts is style transfer. By leveraging the power of AI algorithms, artists can transform their artwork's style while preserving its content. Style transfer algorithms analyze the stylistic elements of existing artwork and apply those characteristics to new images. This process enables artists to reimagine their work in different artistic styles, emphasizing specific aesthetics or themes. Not only does style transfer enhance the visual appeal of concept arts, but it also encourages experimentation and enables artists to explore new artistic directions.

Another remarkable advancement in the realm of AI-assisted concept arts is the use of Generative Adversarial Networks (GANs). GANs are a powerful framework that involves a generator model and a discriminator model working in tandem. The generator learns to produce new images, while the discriminator learns to distinguish between real and generated images. Through a competitive process of training and feedback, GANs can generate highly realistic images that blur the line between human creations and AI-generated content.

GANs have facilitated the creation of AI-generated concept arts, where artists can collaborate with AI algorithms to generate new ideas and expand their creative horizons. By inputting a set of initial parameters or concepts, GANs can generate a variety of visual outputs, providing artists with a wealth of inspiration. This symbiotic relationship between human creativity and AI capabilities not only streamlines the artistic process but also introduces fresh and exciting perspectives to the world of concept arts.

Moreover, AI and ML also contribute to the concept arts domain through semantic understanding and content analysis. AI algorithms can analyze and interpret the elements within an artwork, such as objects, scenes, and emotions, enabling artists to gain valuable insights into the visual composition. This semantic understanding assists artists in refining their artwork, ensuring that it effectively conveys their intended message or narrative. Additionally, content analysis techniques can facilitate the organization and retrieval of vast archives of visual resources, aiding artists in finding relevant references and expanding their creative repertoire.

As AI and ML continue to evolve, the integration of

these technologies into the concept arts landscape holds immense potential. From automated colorization and image enhancement to intelligent design assistance and personalized artwork recommendations, AI-driven tools can empower artists to amplify their artistic expression and redefine the limits of their creative capabilities.

Example 3:

Prompts: "A majestic blue heron stands gracefully next to the water as the sun sets. The scene is rendered in a detailed and lifelike manner, capturing the intricate beauty of the heron's feathers and the shimmering water drops. The color palette consists of light crimson and gray tones, creating a serene atmosphere. The artwork is created using advanced 3D technology, showcasing the baroque elegance of the animal."

Created using Gencraft.com

Style : watercolor

Model: Amazing details

Prompts inspiration was taken from https:// vitalentum.net/

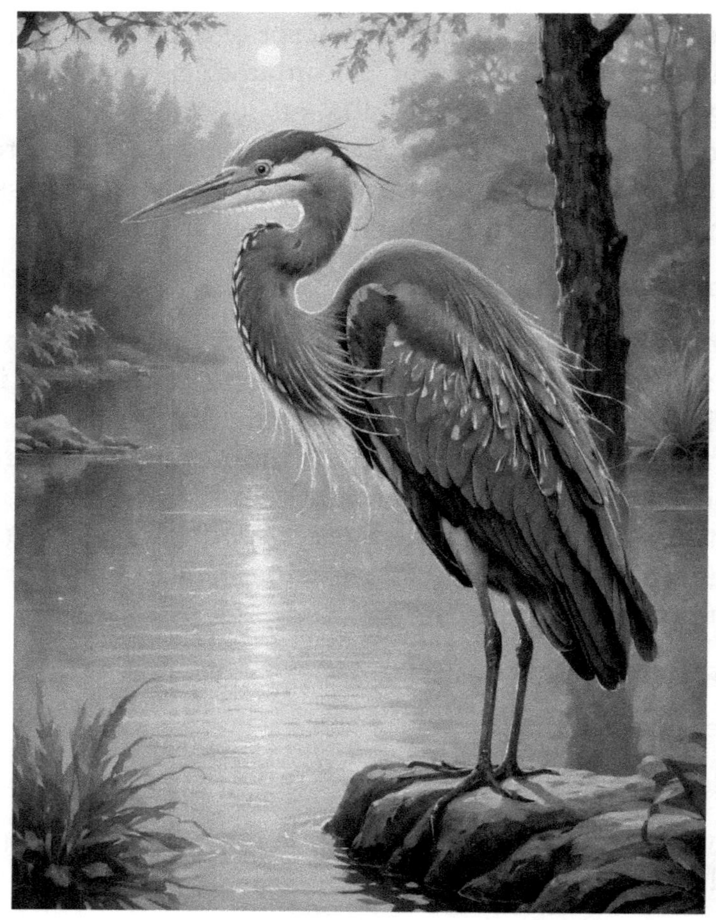

Intricate beauty of the heron's feathers v1

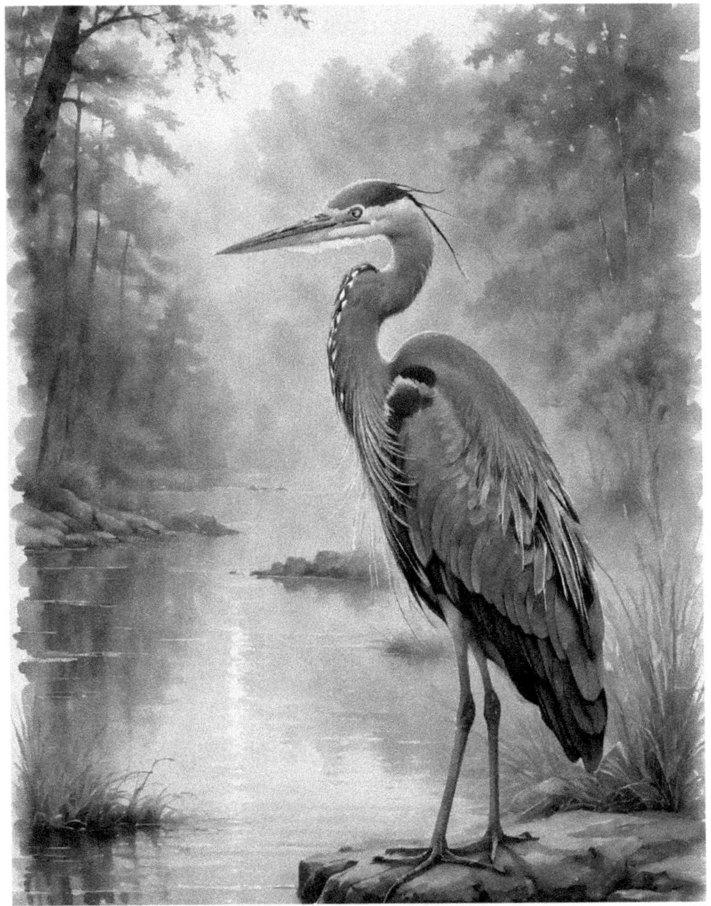

Intricate beauty of the heron's feathers v2

In conclusion, the fusion of AI and ML with concept arts has paved the way for unprecedented possibilities in the creative realm. By harnessing the power of AI algorithms, artists and designers can transcend traditional boundaries and unlock new avenues of artistic exploration. Through style transfer, GANs, and semantic understanding, AI-assisted concept arts foster a harmonious collaboration between human creativity and machine learning prowess. As we continue our journey into the realm of AI-enhanced concept arts, let us embrace the opportunities that await, where the imagination knows no bounds and creativity flourishes with the assistance of intelligent algorithms.

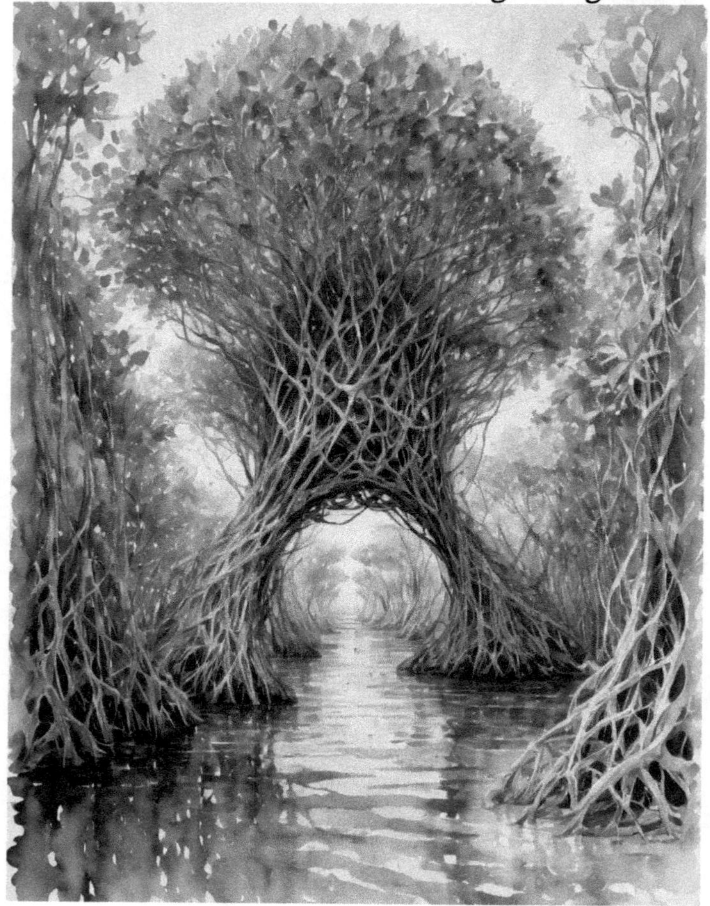

CHAPTER 3: UTILIZING ALGORITHMS IN CONCEPT ART CREATION

Concept art, the visual representation of ideas, plays a fundamental role in various creative industries such as gaming, film, and advertising. It serves as the blueprint for bringing imagination to life. Over the years, the utilization of algorithms has revolutionized the field of concept art creation, enabling artists to enhance their creativity and efficiency like never before.

In this chapter, we will explore various algorithms and their applications in concept art creation. From generative algorithms to style transfer and content synthesis, these computational tools have augmented the artist's toolbox, unlocking new possibilities and pushing the boundaries of visual expression.

Generative algorithms, one of the most exciting advancements in concept art, have transformed the creative process. By utilizing machine learning techniques, these algorithms are trained on vast amounts of data, allowing them to generate original and diverse concepts automatically. Through the analysis of existing artworks, textures, and color schemes, generative algorithms can propose new ideas and compositions that fuel the artist's inspiration. This symbiotic relationship between human creativity and machine learning offers endless opportunities for unique and compelling concept art.

Style transfer is another powerful algorithmic technique that aids in concept art creation. By extracting the visual style from one image and applying it to another, artists can seamlessly blend different artistic influences and create captivating visual compositions.

The ability to transfer the style of a traditional painting onto a futuristic concept or the aesthetics of a comic book onto a realistic scene opens up new realms of creative exploration. Style transfer algorithms provide artists with a versatile tool to experiment with various visual languages, creating a rich and diverse range of concept art styles.

Content synthesis algorithms, on the other hand, provide artists with the ability to generate complex scenes automatically. By inputting a basic description or a rough sketch, these algorithms analyze the provided information and generate detailed imagery, complete with objects, environments, and lighting. This technique enables artists to quickly iterate and explore different design possibilities, saving valuable time while maintaining creative control. Content synthesis algorithms empower artists to focus more on the ideation process, allowing them to dive deeper into their concepts and explore alternative visual directions.

The integration of algorithms in concept art creation not only enhances the artist's capabilities but also inspires fresh, innovative ideas. By combining human imagination with the computational power of algorithms, artists can break free from artistic constraints and tap into uncharted creative territories. From intricate character designs to immersive environments, the impact of algorithmic tools in concept art is undeniable.

The infusion of algorithms into the realm of concept art not only amplifies the artist's abilities but also serves as a wellspring of inspiration for novel and innovative ideas. The synergy between human imagination and the computational prowess of algorithms allows artists to transcend traditional constraints, unlocking unexplored realms of creativity. Whether crafting detailed character designs or immersive environments, the influence of algorithmic tools on concept art is profound.

Thanks to the advent of AI generatives, individuals with creative ideas seeking to experiment with concept art now have the opportunity to explore the artistic capabilities of platforms like Gencraft or Prompthunt. These tools empower anyone to venture into the realm of creating aesthetically pleasing art pieces, ushering in a new era of accessibility and creative expression.

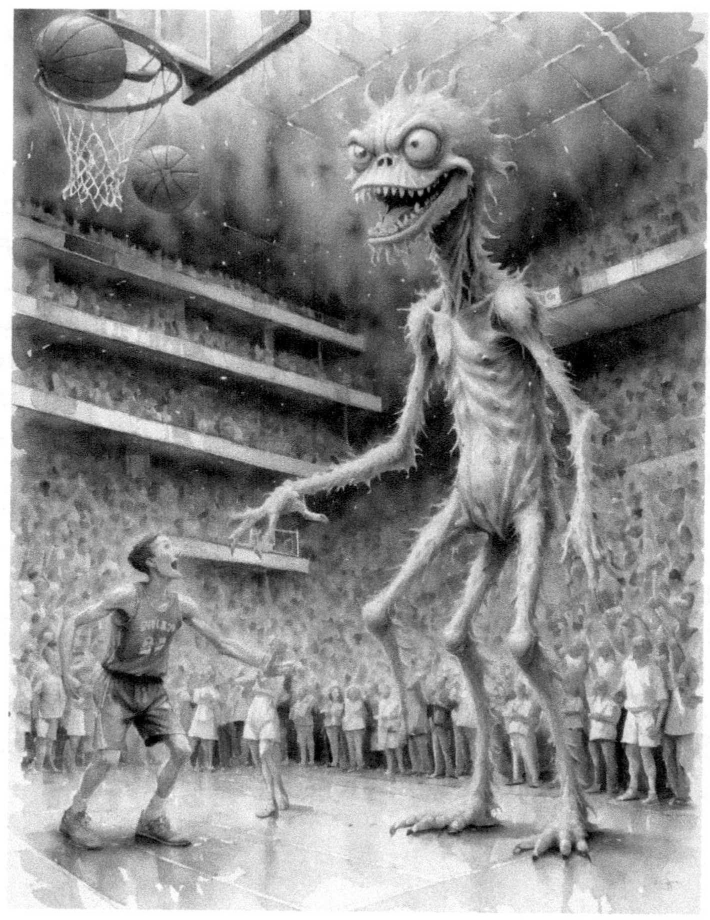

Procedural content generation (PCG) algorithms provide artists with a powerful tool for generating vast and varied landscapes, environments, and objects. By utilizing mathematical functions and randomization, these algorithms can automatically create intricate and diverse designs with minimal effort. PCG algorithms allow artists to quickly generate intricate cities, detailed terrains, realistic foliage, and complex architectural structures. This not only saves valuable time but also enables artists to explore new design possibilities by experimenting with different parameters and configurations.

Moreover, PCG algorithms provide a level of realism and complexity that would be almost impossible to achieve manually, making them invaluable for concept artists working on large-scale projects or immersive worlds.

In addition to PCG, photo-realistic rendering algorithms have revolutionized the way concept art is visualized and presented. These algorithms utilize advanced ray tracing techniques and lighting simulations to create stunning, lifelike imagery that rivals traditional photography.

By accurately simulating the behavior of light as it interacts with different materials and environments, photo-realistic rendering algorithms can produce highly detailed and realistic renders.

This allows concept artists to showcase their ideas with unparalleled visual fidelity, helping clients and collaborators to truly envision the potential of their concepts.

Furthermore, these algorithms can be used to explore different lighting conditions, camera angles, and even simulate the passage of time, providing artists with a versatile set of tools for presenting their concepts in the most compelling and realistic way possible.

As technology continues to evolve, interactive concept art has emerged as an exciting new frontier for concept artists. By incorporating interactive elements into their artwork, artists can engage viewers on a deeper level and offer immersive experiences. Interactive concept art can take various forms, such as virtual reality experiences, augmented reality overlays, or even interactive installations.

These algorithms empower artists to create dynamic and interactive narratives, where viewers can actively engage with the concept art, explore different angles, or even influence the outcome of the artwork itself.

This interactive element not only captivates audiences but also allows for a more personal and emotional connection with the concept, further enhancing its impact and memorability.

The integration of these advanced algorithmic techniques in concept art creation opens up endless possibilities for artists to express their vision and push creative boundaries. Whether it's the generation of vast landscapes and complex environments, the creation of photo-realistic renders, or the incorporation of interactivity, algorithms have become indispensable tools in the artist's toolbox.

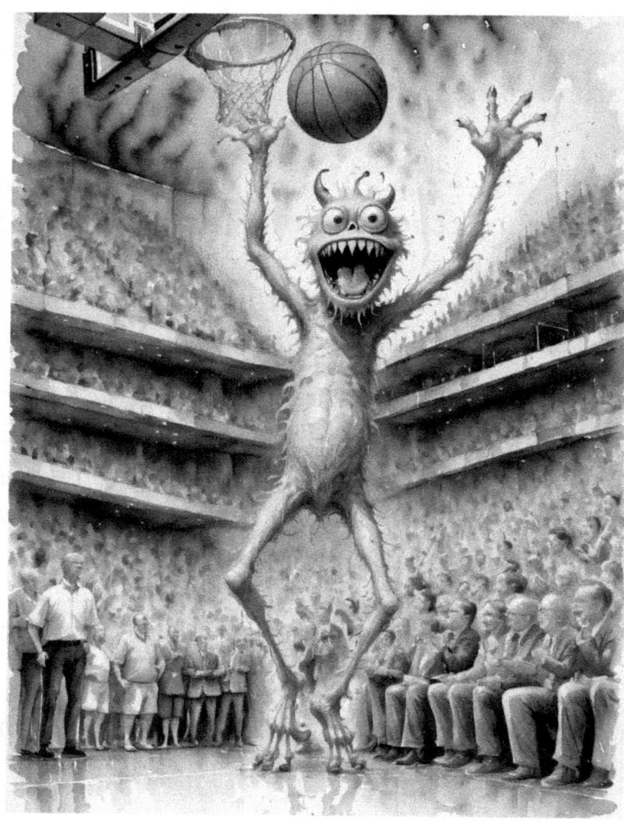

In conclusion, the second half of this chapter has shed light on the transformative power of procedural content generation, photo-realistic rendering, and interactive concept art. By harnessing the potential of these algorithmic advancements, concept artists can unlock new realms of creativity and immerse audiences in captivating visual experiences. As the field of algorithmic concept art continues to evolve, it is essential for artists to embrace these technologies and utilize them as powerful allies in their creative journeys. Join us as we delve deeper into the intricacies of these algorithms and uncover the secrets behind their application in concept art creation.

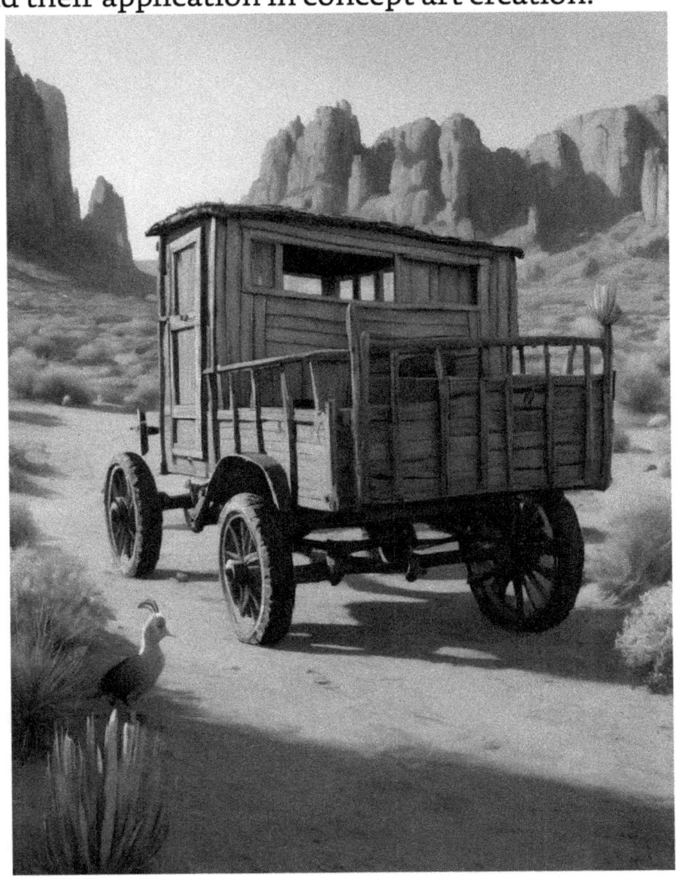

CHAPTER 4: ENHANCING CONCEPT ART TECHNIQUES WITH AI

Traditional concept art techniques have long been cherished by artists, serving as the foundation for breathtaking visuals in films, video games, and various forms of visual media. However, with the recent advancements in artificial intelligence (AI), new opportunities have emerged to enhance and automate these techniques, pushing the boundaries of creativity even further.

One aspect where AI has shown remarkable capabilities is the rendering of lighting and color in concept art. Lighting plays a crucial role in setting the mood and atmosphere of a piece, and AI algorithms can assist artists in achieving their desired effects effortlessly.

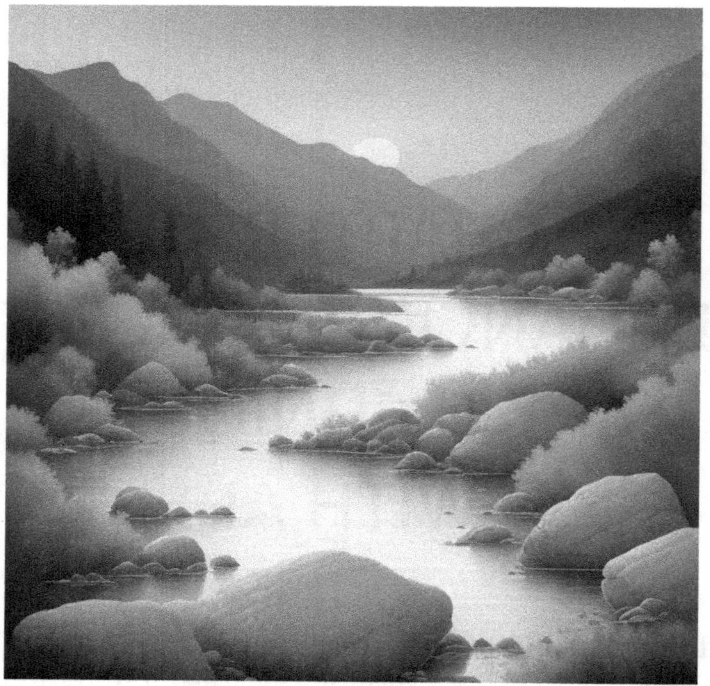

By analyzing existing concept art and learning from a vast array of reference images, AI algorithms can generate lighting suggestions that align with the artist's vision.

These suggestions act as a starting point, providing artists with inspiration and allowing them to focus on refining and adding personal touches to the final artwork.

In addition to lighting, AI algorithms have also proven invaluable in the domain of composition analysis.

The arrangement of visual elements holds immense importance in concept art, as it guides the viewer's gaze and enhances storytelling. With the help of AI, artists can now receive feedback on their compositions and make informed decisions to improve the overall impact of their artwork.

By analyzing established rules of composition and recognizing patterns in successful concept art, AI algorithms can provide suggestions and alternative compositions tailored to the artist's intentions.

Character design is another area greatly influenced by AI. Creating compelling and visually striking characters requires a deep understanding of proportions, anatomy, and aesthetic preferences.

AI-based tools can assist artists in this process by providing references, generating variations, and even offering specific details based on a given description.

Utilizing AI in character design allows artists to explore new possibilities without being bound by preconceived notions, fostering creativity and enabling the birth of unique and captivating characters.

Moreover, AI can expedite the iterative process of concept art, allowing artists to experiment with different ideas, styles, and visual elements in a shorter amount of time. This accelerated workflow empowers artists to focus on the creative aspects while relying on AI to handle repetitive tasks and generate alternative suggestions.

As a result, artists can explore a wider range of possibilities, iterate more extensively, and ultimately create artwork that exceeds their initial expectations.

The integration of AI into traditional concept art techniques is a testament to the continuous evolution of artistic expression.

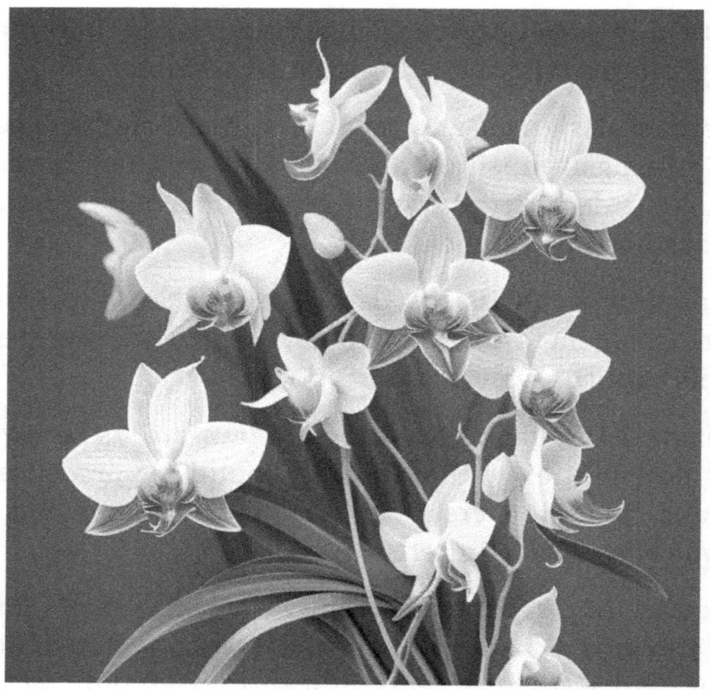

While some may fear that this technological advancement will replace human creativity and diminish the role of artists, it is important to understand that AI acts as a tool, an extension of the artist's hand.

The true essence of art lies within the artist's imagination and emotional connection to their work, which no algorithm can replicate. Instead, AI serves as a collaborative partner, augmenting the artist's skills and opening doors to new artistic frontiers.

As technology continues to evolve, artists and enthusiasts alike eagerly anticipate the second half of this chapter, which will delve deeper into the specific AI techniques and tools available to enhance the world of concept art.

The possibilities are boundless, and the impact of AI on the artistic landscape is just beginning to unfold.

Brace yourself for a journey into the realm of AI-assisted

concept art, as we explore the depths of its potential and witness the seamless fusion of human creativity and artificial intelligence in action.

One of the remarkable AI techniques that have revolutionized concept art is style transfer. Style transfer algorithms analyze a variety of reference images and learn their unique artistic styles.

These algorithms then enable artists to apply those styles to their own concept art, instantly transforming the artwork to mimic the aesthetic of renowned artists or even iconic art movements. This technique opens up possibilities for experimentation and allows artists to explore different visual styles effortlessly.

Another valuable aspect of AI in concept art lies in texture generation.

Traditionally, creating intricate and detailed textures required painstaking effort and time-consuming processes. However, with the advent of AI, artists can now generate complex textures automatically, saving valuable time and allowing them to focus on the larger scope of their artwork.

By training algorithms on vast databases of textures, AI can produce high-quality and realistic textures that seamlessly integrate with the overall concept.

Furthermore, AI has become an indispensable tool for generating landscapes and backgrounds in concept art.

Creating realistic and immersive environments often demands extensive knowledge of perspective, lighting, and natural elements.

AI algorithms can assist artists in this process by generating realistic landscapes based on a few simple inputs or references.

Artists can then manipulate and refine these generated landscapes to fit their artistic vision, empowering them to create vast and imaginative worlds.

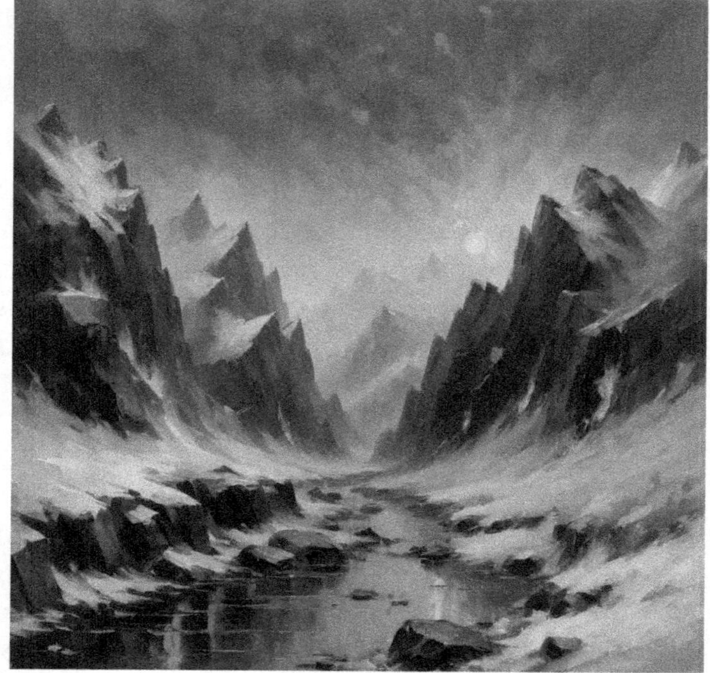

In addition to enhancing traditional techniques, AI can also enable entirely new creative avenues in concept art.

Generative Adversarial Networks (GANs) have gained popularity in recent years for their ability to generate entirely new and unique content.

GANs consist of two neural networks—one that generates content (the generator) and another that judges its quality (the discriminator).

Over time, these networks learn from each other, resulting in the creation of previously unseen and diverse concept art.

This AI technique not only pushes the boundaries of creativity but also helps artists overcome creative blocks and discover novel ideas.

However, as AI continues to advance in the world of concept art, it is crucial to maintain the balance between human creativity and technological assistance.

While AI can automate certain aspects of the artistic process, it is the artist's unique perspective, imagination, and emotional connection to their work that bring life to the artwork.

The true essence of art lies in the human touch, and AI should always serve as a tool rather than a replacement for authentic creativity.

The integration of AI into concept art is an exciting and ongoing journey, where traditional techniques merge with cutting-edge technology.

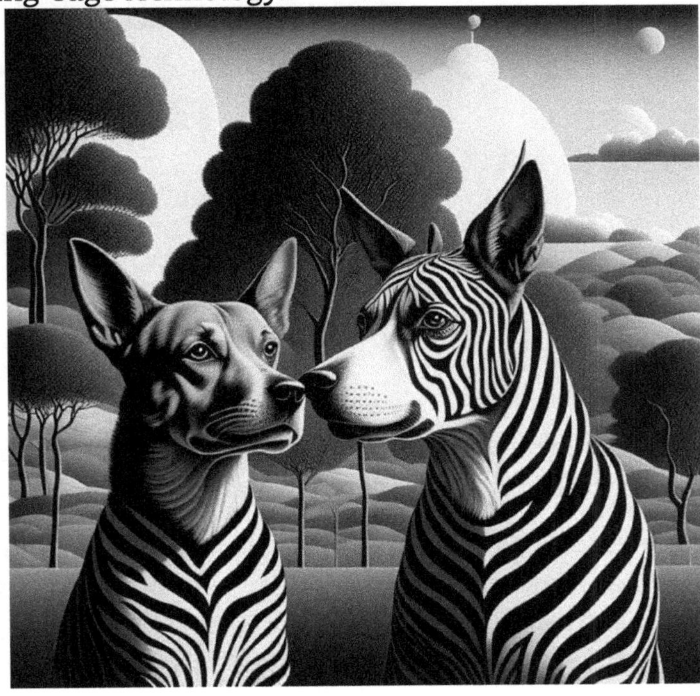

As artists and enthusiasts, we are witnessing a new era of artistry, fueled by AI-assisted techniques that push the boundaries of imagination and aesthetics. The possibilities are endless, and the only limitation is the artist's own vision.

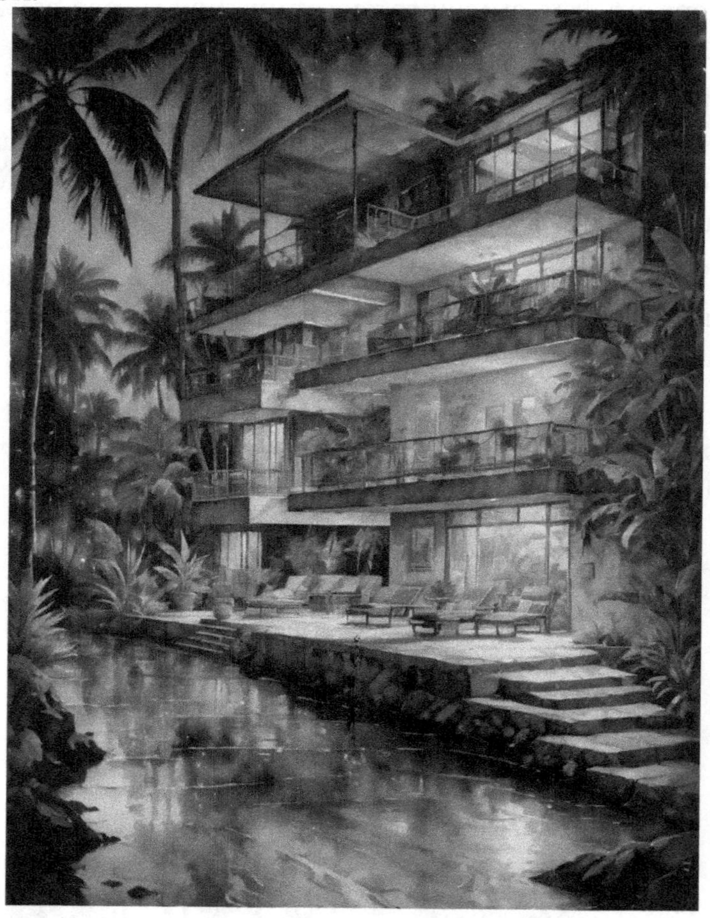

In conclusion, the world of concept art is being enhanced and transformed by the powerful capabilities of AI.

Lighting and color rendering, composition analysis, character design, texture generation, landscape creation, and innovative AI techniques like style transfer and GANs are all revolutionizing the concept art process. By embracing AI as a partner in the creative journey, artists can explore new frontiers, overcome limitations, and bring their artistic visions to life in ways never before imagined.

The collaboration of human imagination and artificial intelligence is propelling the art of algorithms to new heights, and the future holds immense potential for the fusion of technology and creativity.

Dream big, create fearlessly, and let the art of algorithms guide you on a remarkable journey of artistic discovery.

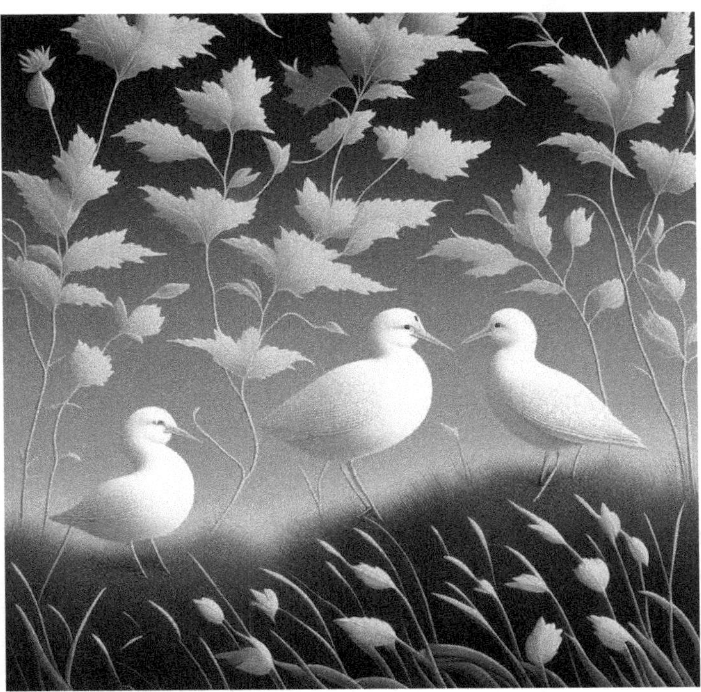

CHAPTER 5: ETHICAL CONSIDERATIONS AND FUTURE POSSIBILITIES

Artificial Intelligence (AI) has revolutionized many aspects of our daily lives, and the world of concept art is no exception. As we delve into the ethical considerations surrounding the use of AI in concept art, we also uncover the exciting possibilities that lie ahead for the future of AI-powered artistic creations.

The integration of AI into the realm of concept art invites us to reflect on the ethical implications of this technological convergence. One of the primary concerns is the potential loss of human creativity and originality.

Will AI-powered algorithms replace the need for human artists, causing a decline in the value placed on handmade art?

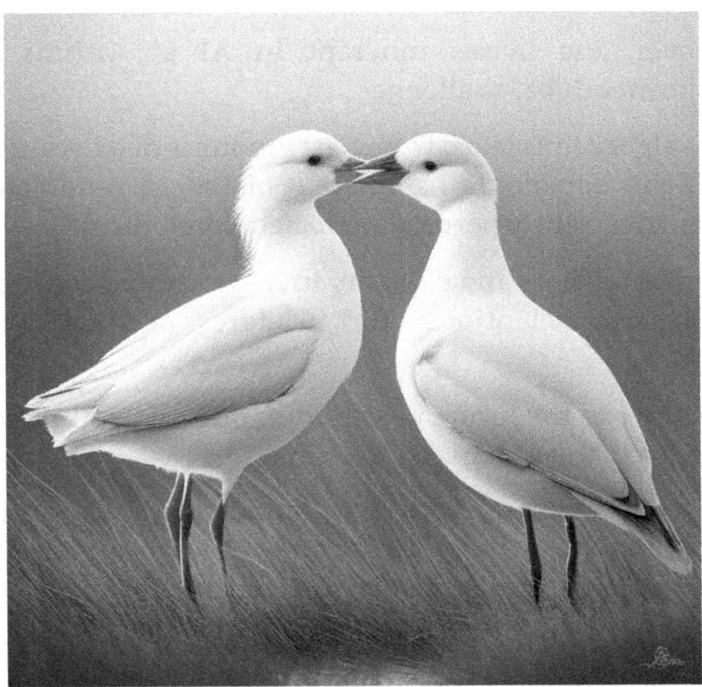

Critics argue that relying on AI for artistic creation may result in a homogenization of ideas and aesthetics.

Without the nuances of the human touch, will the art world become saturated with repetitive and generic pieces?

However, proponents argue that AI can serve as a powerful tool to enhance and augment human creativity, fostering new forms of artistic expression.

Another ethical consideration is the issue of intellectual property rights. Concept art often serves as a foundation for various forms of media, such as films, video games, and advertisements.

When AI algorithms generate concept art, who holds the rights to these creations?

Should it be the human artist who trained the AI, the AI itself, or perhaps a combination of both?

Moreover, the biases inherent in AI algorithms pose significant ethical challenges.

These algorithms learn from vast amounts of existing data, and if this data contains inherent biases, AI-generated art may inadvertently perpetuate societal prejudices.

Ensuring fairness and diversity in AI-generated concept art requires a conscientious effort to address and rectify these biases.

Nevertheless, the future possibilities offered by AI-powered concept art are undeniably exciting.

The collaboration between human artists and AI algorithms has the potential to unleash unparalleled creativity and unlock new artistic frontiers.

By leveraging the computational power of AI, artists can explore unimaginable possibilities and transcend the boundaries of their individual capabilities.

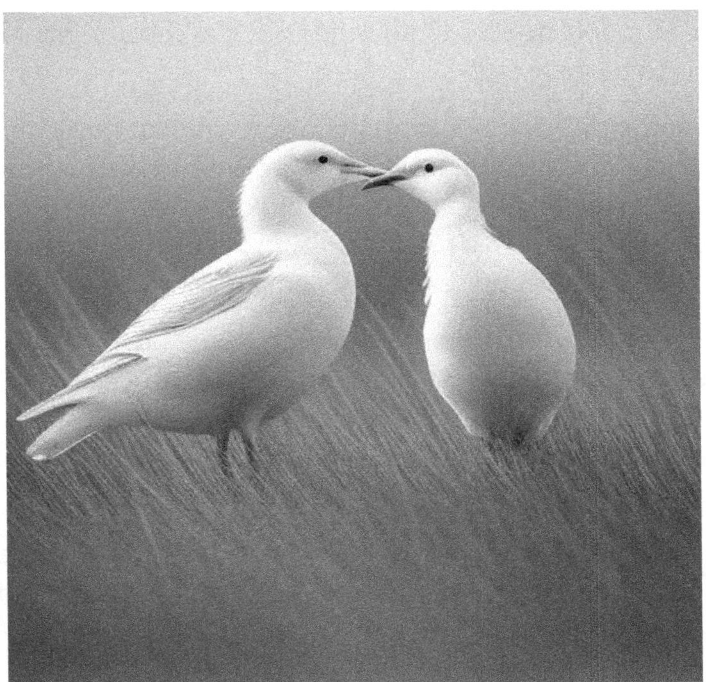

AI algorithms can assist artists in tasks such as generating initial concepts, exploring various styles, and even predicting audience preferences.

This collaboration between human intuition and AI automation brings forth a synergy that melds the best of both worlds.

The artist becomes the conductor, guiding the artistic process, while the AI algorithms act as the instrumentalists, enhancing and elevating the final artistic output.

The future of AI-powered artistic creations holds promises and surprises yet to be fully realized. As technology advances, we may witness the emergence of AI-generated art that is indistinguishable from human-made art, blurring the line between man and machine. The ability of AI algorithms to mimic specific artistic styles and even recreate masterpieces challenges our perception of what it means to be an artist.

In conclusion, the ethical considerations surrounding the use of AI in concept art cannot be overlooked. We must address issues of creativity, intellectual property rights, and biases to ensure a responsible and inclusive integration of AI into the artistic realm.

Simultaneously, the possibilities that lie ahead with AI-powered artistic creations are awe-inspiring, bringing us to the forefront of a new era in art. Exciting times await as we navigate the intricate landscapes where human imagination and AI ingenuity converge.

One of the primary concerns surrounding the integration of AI into concept art is the potential devaluation of handmade art and the role of human artists.

Critics argue that AI algorithms may replace the need for human creativity, leading to a decline in the value placed on traditional artistic skills.

This fear is not entirely unfounded, as the development of AI technologies continues to advance at an astonishing pace.

However, proponents argue that rather than replacing human artists, AI can serve as a powerful tool to enhance and augment their creative capabilities.

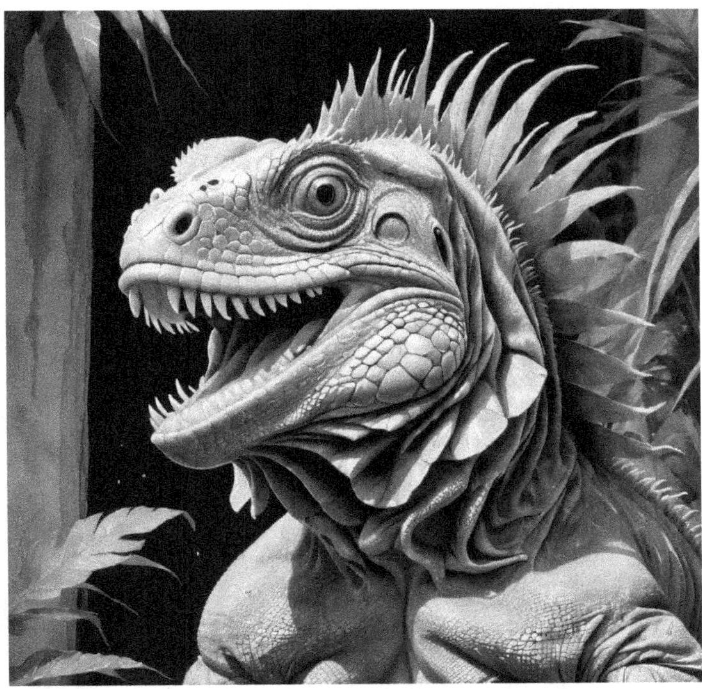

The integration of AI into concept art raises questions about intellectual property rights. When AI algorithms generate concept art, determining who holds the rights to these creations becomes a complex issue.

Some argue that credit should be given to the human artist who trained the AI, as they are responsible for the overall design and aesthetic choices.

Others argue that the AI itself should be recognized as a co-creator, given its significant role in generating the final artwork.

Ultimately, finding a balanced approach that acknowledges both human and AI contributions while respecting intellectual property rights will be crucial in navigating this new artistic landscape.

Another ethical consideration lies in the biases inherent within AI algorithms. These algorithms learn from vast amounts of existing data, which may contain societal biases. Consequently, AI-generated concept art can inadvertently perpetuate and reinforce these biases, further exacerbating inequality and excluding marginalized perspectives.

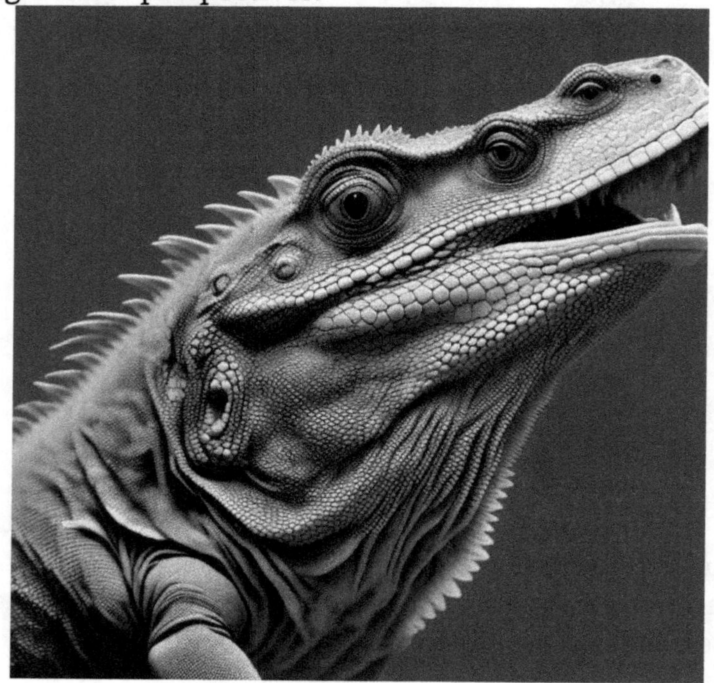

Addressing this issue requires a conscientious effort to continuously evaluate and rectify biases in the training data, ensuring fairness, diversity, and inclusivity in AI-generated artistic creations.

Despite these ethical challenges, AI-powered concept art offers exciting future possibilities. The collaboration between human artists and AI algorithms has the potential to unleash unparalleled creativity and unlock new artistic frontiers.

By leveraging AI's computational power, artists can push beyond the boundaries of their individual capabilities, exploring unfamiliar styles and pushing the limits of their artistic expression. AI algorithms can assist in generating initial concepts, suggesting variations, and predicting audience preferences, opening up new avenues for artistic exploration.

This synergy between human intuition and AI automation brings forth a symbiotic relationship between the artist and the AI algorithms.

The artist becomes the conductor, guiding the artistic process, while the AI algorithms act as instrumentalists, enhancing and elevating the final artistic output. This collaboration enables artists to create works that would have been challenging or even impossible to achieve solely through human means.

Looking forward, the future of AI-powered artistic creations holds promises and surprises yet to be fully realized.

As technology advances, we may witness AI-generated art that is indistinguishable from human-made art, blurring the line between man and machine.

The ability of AI algorithms to mimic specific artistic styles and recreate masterpieces challenges our perception of what it means to be an artist.

This opens up new realms of creativity and self-expression, inviting artists to explore uncharted territories and redefine the parameters of artistic achievement.

In conclusion, the integration of AI into the realm of concept art brings forth a unique set of ethical considerations that must be addressed responsibly. By addressing concerns surrounding human creativity, intellectual property rights, and biases, we can ensure an inclusive and meaningful integration of AI into the artistic landscape.

Simultaneously, the possibilities that lie ahead with AI-powered artistic creations are awe-inspiring, propelling us into a new era of art.

Embracing this journey where human imagination and AI ingenuity converge, we stand at the precipice of exciting times in the world of concept art and beyond.

CHAPTER 6: ENDLESS POSSIBILITY

This is an opportunity open to everyone, whether you're an artist, a student, or an entrepreneur. It's a chance to swiftly bring your ideas to life, unlocking new realms of exploration and igniting innovative concepts through the use of AI tools.

Moreover, it provides an avenue for those interested in generating a side income from Digital Art—create captivating pieces, print, frame, and sell them to collectors or homeowners.

Start by showcasing your creations within your friend circle, community, or affiliated groups; the potential is limitless.

Find all the applications and websites mentioned in this book via the provided links. Enjoy your creative journey, and if you find this resource valuable, we'd be grateful for a five-star review. Thank you for your support.

Leverage the Prompts writing ideas from this website, each image shows the prompt content was used: https://vitalentum.net/ai/43259.html

Insert prompts into any of these websites for best result

https://www.prompthunt.com/ (use Magic Enhancer for different version of the image)

or

https://gencraft.com/

or

https://leonardo.ai/

We used this prompt on Prompthunt, check out the below 12 marvelous results.

"high quality, 8K Ultra HD, Imagine a vibrant canvas illuminated by a cascade of colorful binary code, forming the silhouette of a captivating woman, The dynamic lines and patterns, reminiscent of a digital dance, weave together to create a harmonious fusion of technology and art, The binary code, in hues ranging from electric blues to radiant reds and vivid greens, breathes life into the woman's form, Her silhouette emerges as a synthesis of the digital and the organic, a testament to the seamless integration of technology and beauty in your masterful creation, by Yuki Sakura, high detailed"

Theme: Watercolor

Magic Enhancer 2 times

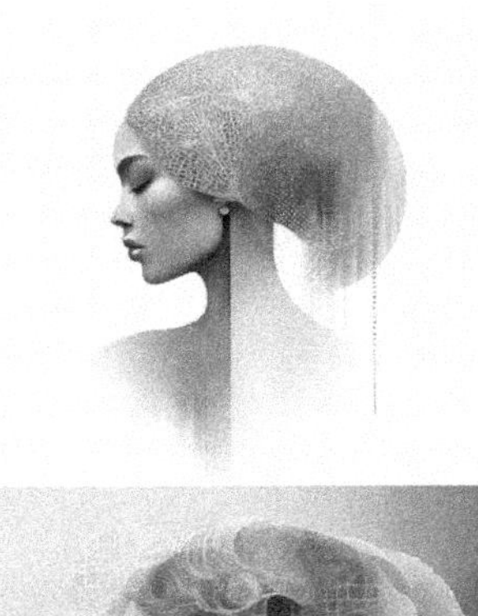

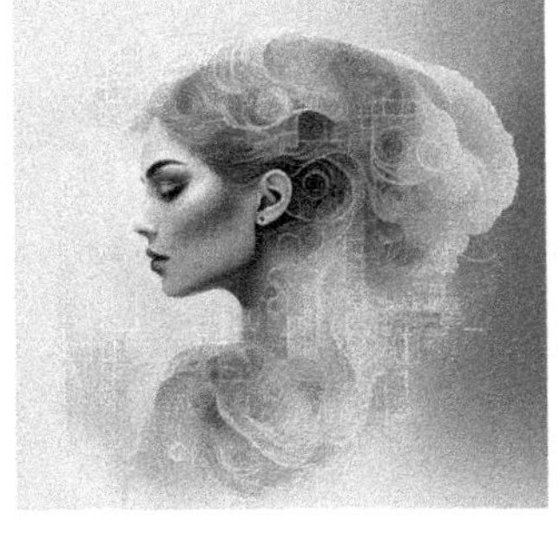

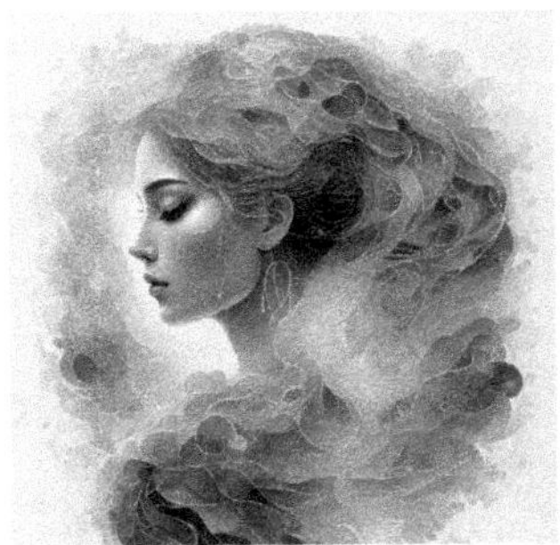

Theme: Surrealism

Magic Enhancer 2 times

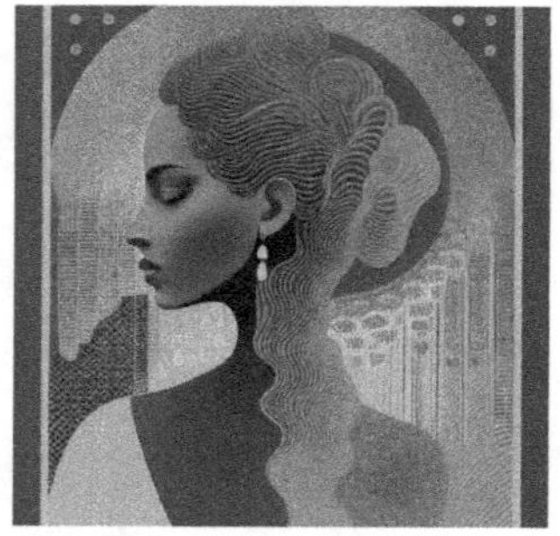

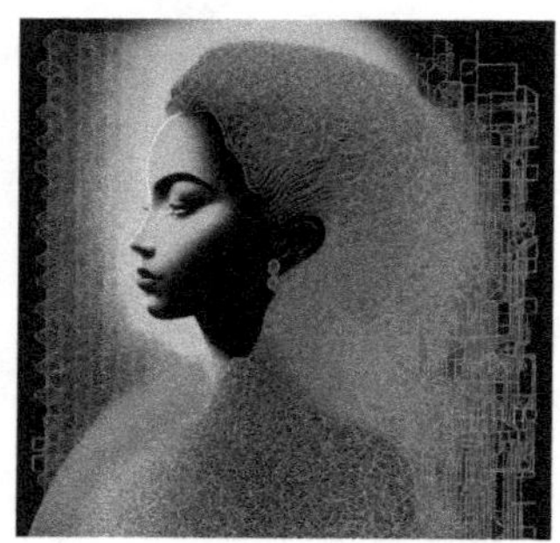

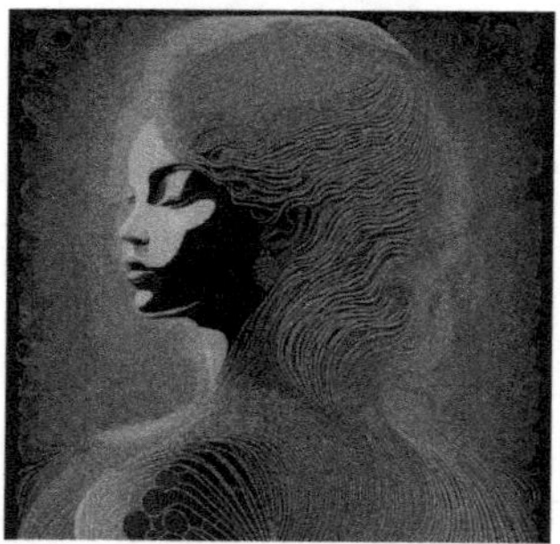

Theme: Cinematic

Magic Enhancer 2 times

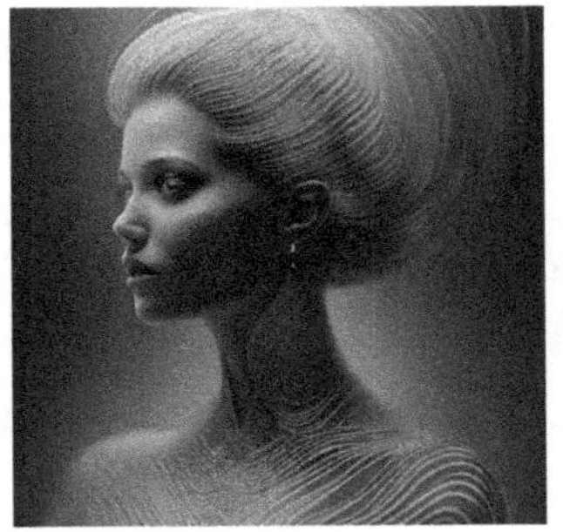

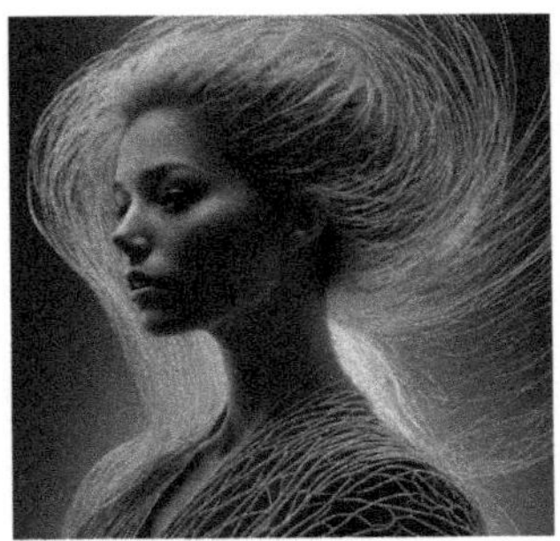

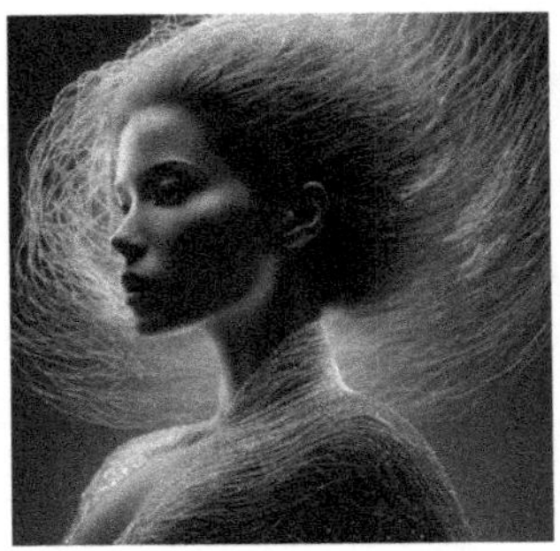

Theme: Doodles

Magic Enhancer 2 times

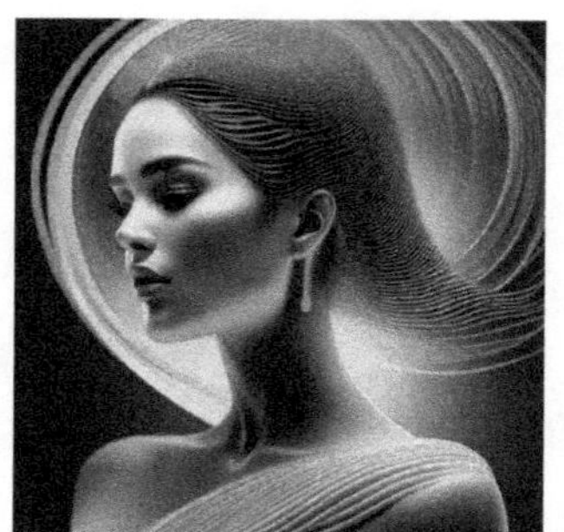

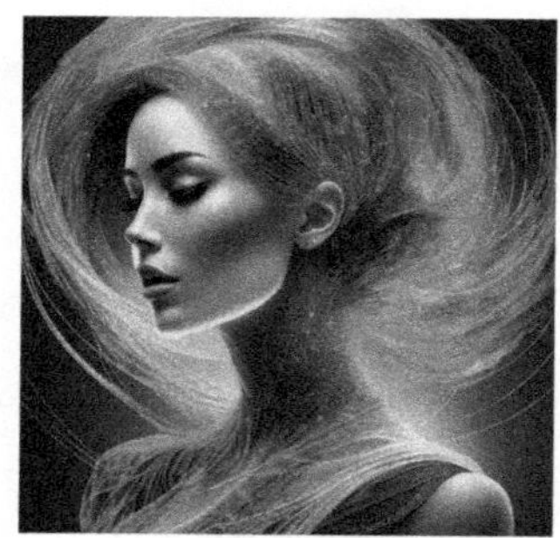

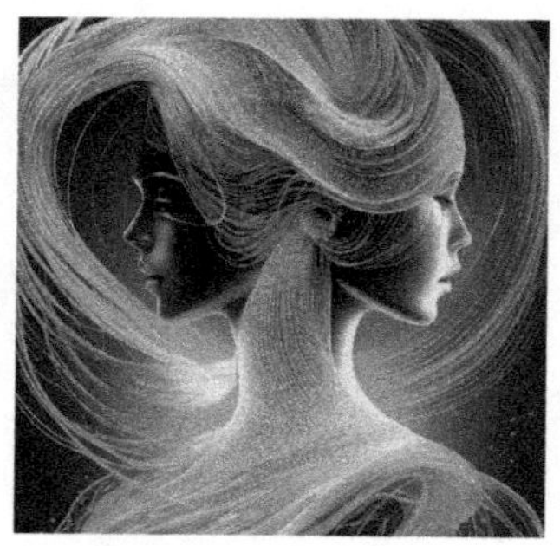

CONCLUSION

Concept art is the creative backbone for diverse industries, serving as a vital bridge between imagination and realization in gaming, film, and advertising.

The integration of algorithms has transformed the concept art landscape, empowering artists to reach unprecedented levels of creativity and efficiency. Reflecting on the journey through concept art and algorithms reveals boundless potential for artistic expression.

The ability to customize prompt samples offers endless possibilities, allowing artists to craft tailored concept arts. In this dynamic intersection of human creativity and algorithms, the message is clear: the sky is the limit.

Artists now possess tools that not only enhance their capabilities but also encourage pushing the boundaries of what's conceivable.

ABOUT THE AUTHOR

Lily Ravioli

The combination of artistic vision with computational power has empowered artists and anyone to elevate their creativity and efficiency to unprecedented heights. As we reflect on the journey through the realms of concept art and algorithms, it becomes clear that the potential for artistic expression knows no bounds. The ability to 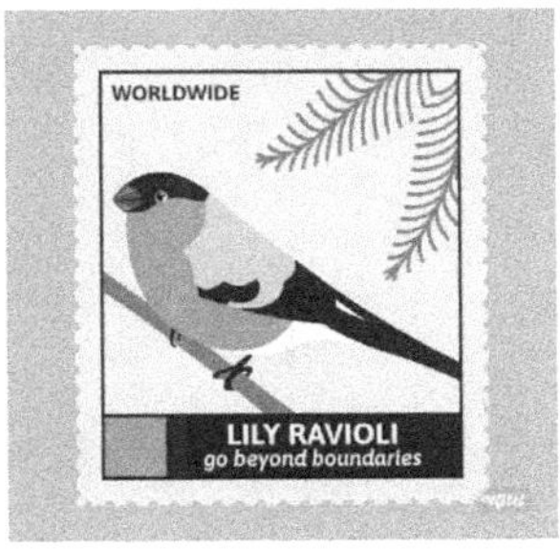

tweak and mold prompt samples into unique, personalized versions opens up a world of endless possibilities. With each variation, artists can craft concept arts and images tailored precisely to their vision and needs. Indeed, the horizon stretches as far as the imagination can reach.

Thanks for your support and have a blessed day!